Grains of my Heart

Kory Avila

BookLeaf Publishing

India | USA | UK

Presentation by *BookLeaf Publishing*

Web: www.bookleafpub.com

E-mail: info@bookleafpub.com

ISBN: 9789360945558

First edition 2024

This book is dedicated to the person who believed in me, when I didn't.

PREFACE

I have finally decided to share my poetry with the universe. I want to share these moments that I created into poetry. Something that has truly helped me get through my days is writing and creating a safe space for others who cannot put their emotions into words sometimes. For the lovers of poetry, the believers and the ones who stay up at night and think; I hope my writing touches your heart too.

Tennessee Whiskey

Your love is like Tennessee whiskey; it goes down smoothly and touches my soul. Once a drop touches my lips, the sensation through my bones quiver.
Still, speechless. Your love in this cup is unbound.
You keep me safe and i'll keep you wild.
You touched me before you ever touched me.
Like Tennessee whiskey, your love is timeless.

Brother

Brother, I wish you can see the world through my eyes. Nothing is what it seems. When I look at you, I see a little boy smiling back at me. Your eyes still light up at the sound of our mother's voice. I will be your lighthouse for always. Take my hand when you are sad. I will hold you even when it feels like you're slipping away. I will find you in the dark, and sit with you until the sun rises again. Brother.

Time

Time is strange.
You think if it keeps passing by, that you will
forget.
Time is a thief.
I don't want to remember you. But time and time
again, reminds me of what was.
I see you everywhere, but more in my dreams.
I still see you when I close my eyes. Your face is
imprinted on the bottom of my eyelids.
I still search for you in a crowded room.
Time goes by, and I still hear your laugh.
You aren't here, but why can I still feel you?
You left but time stood still.

Waves

Waves of life pass us by, like the breeze in the
wind.
Sometimes crashing down or staying afloat
above water.
Hard to tell if the waves will stay high or low; or
sink into the grains of sand.
Waves of joy turn into grief.
Grief becomes a slow burn.
That burn turns into a rage of flames.
Tears overflow on the curves of one's face to put
out the fire.
Then what?
Joy comes again.

Lost

5

You found me at my highest and walked away at
my lowest.
I still searched for you even in the midst of
chaos.
I lost myself in you.
We were once whole but you split us in half.
I made sure to leave a little of my love inside of
you.
Although apart, our souls are somehow, still
intertwined.

Her

Her eyes, shaped like almonds; a chocolate
brown with a light of honey.
Her voice so sweet, yet so slick.
Her presence feels so safe, even in a burning
rage.
Her smile, crooked but beautiful. Her dimples;
deeper than the ocean.
Her laughter, sounds like spring in May.
Her graceful poise with a touch of humility.
Her essence of being is what makes her, her.

Moments

Lately, I have spent my days and nights thinking about where it went wrong. I replay some of my favorite moments of us together, just to feel you again. Those memories are etched on the corners of my mind. I can still you hear you near, yet you're afar. I replay the despairing moments too, almost like a broken record. These moments have stayed. I'm not sure how long they'll linger for, but maybe one day, they'll leave the same way you did.

Rollercoaster

Love is a rollercoaster.
Some days you're up in the air and you're on a
high.
Some days, you get a knot in your stomach and
your hands pressed against your heart.
Some days you're in mid air, and have no time to
catch your breath.
So, you take a risk, and let love be.
Love is a rollercoaster.

Faith

How beautiful is it when you're smiling at
someone, lighting up the room with your eyes?
Yet, no one notices the heaviness in your heart.
Your thoughts weigh on you like bricks on your
shoulders. Aren't you tired? Or will you always
hide behind the curves of your gentle smile?
You're suffocating, but there is still air left.
Catch your breath and walk by faith.

Beautiful child

Beautiful child, don't let go of the dreams you
once had.
You are still capable of flying and touching the
sky.
You grew, but your heart is still the same.
Beautiful child, don't forget how far you have
come.
Remember who you are.

Dream

Each time it rains, I think about the moment we met. It poured down on us and we withered the storm. A million raindrops danced on our heads. You held my hand and we glanced at each other. A familiar feeling; like I have known you in another life. Almost like a dream.

Become

Strangers become friends.
Friends become lovers.
Lovers become enemies.
Enemies become memories of what once was.
Memories become shadows.
Shadows become thoughts.
Thoughts become poetry.

Middle Child

Somewhere between then and now, I think about the joy in my childhood. We didn't have it all, but together, we had everything. The heat came from the oven, as we giggled in the middle of rubbing our hands together. We slept together when darkness became too dark. We made forts out of blankets and called it our home. Sometimes we were lost but together we found a way.

Heaven on Earth

When the heavens call for me, do not be somber.
Like the moon, I will always follow you.
Hold on to our times together on this green
earth.
Hug our memories close to your heart.
Watch the sunrise and know that I will always be
near.

Free

I don't want to go but this is the only way we'll grow.
Spread your wings and be free.
Follow your heart and let the beats of it guide you.
I'll find you again, even if it's just in our dreams.
Be free.

Bit of Hope

The world can be frigid but it can't take the
warmth from my heart.
Passing faces can be cruel to me but it will never
change my vision to their untold pain.
My eyes always see the beauty in the worst.
In the end, the smallest glimmer of hope
overpowers adversity.

Angel mother

I have watched you cry a river of sadness, within
hope.
I have watched you fight silent battles, but they
were loud to my eardrums. Beautifully broken,
yet you still nurtured the best life for I.
You loved me at my lowest.
How can I ever repay you, my Angel mother.

All we have is now

Eventually, the stars in the sky will dim. Everything we ever touched will be gone in dust. All the people we have made laugh will be a small memory, engraved into stone. The only thing that will remain is the undying love we collided with. The type of love that tugged on our heart strings. All our yesterday's will disappear into the depth of the deepest ocean. Tomorrow is a dream away. All we have is now.

Wherever you are

I miss the way the sun would hit your face.
The way the light rays made your eyes glow.
The way the moon reflected into your soul;
making us whole.
I miss the way your head gently fell when you
were tired, or the way your skin pressed against
mine.
I missed the way we chased sunsets and aligned
our smiles with the colors in the sky.
Wherever you are.

Red Rose

You are enough.
You are not too much.
You are the right amount of love.
You are a subtle beauty.
You are not your wounds or mistakes.
You are the epitome of grace.
You are the red rose that grew from the concrete.

Moonlight

The moon knows all my secrets.
I sit under it and watch the way it expands.
I can describe all the shapes of it and the way it
hides behind the clouds.
The moon knows all my secrets.
It watches me go through phases just like itself.
Sometimes whole, sometimes half, but always
there.